Make Money From Your Hobbies

By A Millennial

Spencer C Powell

ISBN: 1544039530
ISBN-13: 978-1544039534

THANK YOU!

Thank you Joe and Carol for putting up with all my shenanigans and "learning opportunities." I know they cost you a lot of money when I was young. It is starting to pay off!

Thank you friends for excusing my frugalness and for letting me practice my hobbies with you.

WHAT YOU'LL NEED TO KNOW:

INTRO

Money is the best. It literally doesn't get any better than money. Well, food, fun and love are pretty great, but money though... I love getting it and I hate spending it. I also love woodworking, but that comes at a price, a price that costs money. If I could craft with the best woods and the coolest tools for free I wouldn't have time to write this book, I would never leave my woodshop. That isn't reality though, or is it? Have you ever wanted to make money from your hobbies? Or would you like to make money from pretty much everything you do in life? I felt the same way, so I started doing it! I make money off pretty much everything I do, well except drink, I'm still working on that one. Maybe I'll buy a liquor store one day... Ok back to hobbies. I want to show you how to sell what you do for fun, and make money from most of your every day tasks.

What is the point of stopping there? Once you are on the money making road, let's take it to the next level! Start a business! We will get your hobby off the ground, making money, and then I will show you what to do next with it. Are you read to turn your skills into a money making machine? Great! Let's get started.

LESSON ONE: EVERYTHING CAN MAKE MONEY

In all of my books I always mention that it isn't how much you make from your job that makes you rich. It is what you do with your money outside of work that makes you wealthy. Wealth is more than just money. Wealth is money, class, and knowledge. I usually tell people to take their money and invest it, but what if instead you spent it on having fun? I don't mean going to the club and dancing every night. I am talking about enjoying a real hobby. Painting, crafting, building, blogging, singing, whatever, they are all great. Everything can make money and it is extremely easy to turn your hobby into a money making machine. I am sure they are great, but I don't think your cardboard coasters will start the next billion-dollar tech company, but they can offset what you spend on making them and they might put some money in your date fund jar.

The other way to make money from what you do as a human is to simply make smart purchases. "Well duhhh Spencer." I mean more than just buying your car or TV at the right price. I am talking about buying everything you own for less than the used market value price. Buying everything you own for less than you can sell it for later. We all own old crap in the garage that we just replaced with new crap. Sell that crap. We will dive into this later on, just know that I am a minimalist and you don't actually need to sell all your sentimental valuables, like I did, to make this work.

I am going to use my own hobbies and purchasing history to tell the story. First, a little background. When I was a teenager I enjoyed two things: swimming and loud speakers. Although I don't own any large speakers anymore and I only look at a pool every 6 months, I think these are some pretty common and reasonable hobbies to have as a teenage boy in the 90's and early 2000's. Naturally, I was a lifeguard to hang by the pool and make some money and I spent all that money on stereo equipment for my awesome 2003 Honda Element. I wanted the biggest and best setup in my car and the

$7.35 an hour just wasn't going to make that happen. What did I have to do to turn my dream into a reality? I had to turn my hobbies into money making opportunities.

Step one was to take swimming to the next level. I was on a competitive swim team and it is tradition for some of the older swimmers to become coaches and teach the younger swimmers what they have learned over the years. I liked this concept, but why make the $10 an hour that the swim team was offering when I could make $60 an hour teaching private lessons? All parents want to see their kids succeed, and they are willing to pay for it. I found out from my own swimming experience that a private coach would charge upwards of $120 an hour to give instructions that I already knew. I made some fliers offering $60 an hour swim lessons and passed them out at swim practices. It was a hit! I started teaching 5 lessons a week. That paid for a lot of speakers and I got to hang around the pool all the time. Hobby, converted.

Buying subwoofers and amplifiers for my car was still a huge waste of money, so I needed a way to turn that around. The key to this was research. Research research research. The internet was my friend, Craigslist and EBay were my best friends. I learned about every speaker company, all of their product lines, and the values of everything they sold. This gave me an edge up on all the listings online. A lot of the time people post things on Craigslist without researching what their items are worth. Even better people post things on Craigslist with a terrible description and nobody is interested because nobody knows what it is. Because I knew the products inside and out, even if the Craigslist listing had a miserable picture, I could most likely determine what it is and what it is worth. I would then be able to find the best deals and nobody else was looking at the same listing. AKA I bought things really really cheap. Unfortunately the cost of car audio doesn't stop at the products used. Installation is expensive. That is unless you know how to do it yourself. Hundreds of YouTube hours later and many failed attempts I learned how to effectively install car audio, avoiding the cost of installation at a shop. Wait, it doesn't sound like I am making any money off of this right? Not yet...

Because I had learned a skill, car audio installation, and I had a product, cheaply purchased speakers and amplifiers, I had the makings of a small business. I started off by purchasing a small audio system. All of the different components were purchased separately and at a great price point. I would then offer the whole setup plus installation at a marked up price, after listening and playing with it for a while of course. People would go for this, it is still cheaper than going to a car audio shop and they didn't know how to install it on their own. After selling and installing my car audio system into someone else's car for a marked up price, I would have a larger amount of money than I originally did. I would then take this money and build an even bigger, nicer setup and repeat the process. This went on until I blew out the electrical system on my beautiful Honda Element with too much bass and my father, thankfully, made me stop. Somehow I still came out on top financially and I got to experience some of the best audio equipment out there. Hobby, converted.

I don't swim or destroy cars with bass anymore but I still have hobbies and I still do them for free. The examples I will use are woodworking and home electronics. I really enjoy building things. I like to make tables and furniture. I should mention, my woodworking, kind of, well, sucks. But it has a purpose. I do it, not to make beautiful pieces of art, but because I like chopping wood up and screwing it back together. It's a hobby remember? If I were some successful carpenter I wouldn't be doing this as a hobby, I'd be selling it to millionaires who like overpriced furniture. I do, however, sell my crappy looking furniture on Craigslist for enough to offset what I pay for it and that is the important part. We can talk about selling practices later.

My other money saving skill is still buying things at the right price. I used to buy things using the knowledge I had of the product but now, I generally use buying power. What do I mean by buying power? Why buy one IPad when you can buy four, sell three of them, and have the fourth one for free or cheap. The other method I use is still similar to what I did as a kid but to the next level. I do what I call offsetting the price. I am always trying new things, like writing books apparently is my new thing. When I get into a new market or product I always do my price research first. If I want a new home stereo, I learn as much as I can about what is available, learn the prices of all those items, find items that are priced below market value, buy them, sell them and come out ahead. An example: I want a new home stereo. I look on Craigslist and find 6 pairs of speakers for sale that are less than their price on EBay(we will go into more detail on how to do all of this later). I buy a pair at an even lower negotiated price, turn around and sell them for a higher price and I am ahead some money. I do this two or three times and finally I have enough money to buy the item I really wanted without spending any cash out of my bank account. This can be done with any product line out there. Now it is time to get dirty with the details. What are your hobbies?

LESSON TWO: THE AVAILABLE MARKETS

So you're sold on offsetting some of the costs your hobby brings on. Maybe you can use that money to become financially independent, or take that money and invest it! Either way you're going to need to know where to buy your hobby supplies and where to sell your end product. That, my friends, is your market. If your hobby is a service, you are limited on the markets you can sell in. If you make something and it is very large, you probably don't want to sell it to someone on the other side of the world because, you know, shipping. It is always important to know who your customer is and where they can find your product. Let's break down some of the big markets and why they should or shouldn't be your best friends.

Local Market:

Your local market includes the people in your neighborhood or even the people in your big city. A lot of the time this market is accessed through friends and family. Your personal network is one of the best ways to reach out to your local market, but there are other ways. Craigslist, which will get its own market category on here, is another way to reach out to these people. Unless you are providing video services over the internet, the local market is pretty much your only option if your hobby is a service. When I taught swim lessons as a teen I couldn't teach lessons to people in California when I was in Colorado, it just makes sense that a service has to be local. Let's say that you love playing piano, you should definitely teach some piano lessons FYI. Call all your local friends and family and tell them that you are teaching lessons and would love to know if anyone they know is interested. Make a Facebook, Twitter, LinkedIn post about your new idea. Put an advertisement on Craigslist. Create fliers and hand them out at events. Make a business card for your service and hand them to people that you meet. Reaching out to your local market is easy and very free. This market is best for services but can also be used for selling a product.

Craigslist:

Craigslist is part of your local market and a resource to reach out to the people around you. Friends and family are always looking to help and you should probably use them, if available, but a lot of times they can't help you with your hobbies. My hobby of building furniture for example needs a larger market than just my friends and family. My friends can only own so many crappy work benches. Craigslist is my best friend! Well, tied with EBay. Craigslist is easy; you log on, create a title, make a little description, and post a picture or two. It doesn't cost anything, it yields results, and it is easy. The key to Craigslist is the pictures. For some reason, people love the crap out of pictures. I think a good description goes a long way, but if you want to sell to the public you need to have a bunch of awesome pictures. Just take your smart phone, walk around the product, and take a picture from each side. Don't post on Craigslist with less than 5 pictures. There is a crazy amount of research out there explaining why more pictures are better but just know that the better your pictures, the more money people are willing to spend on your product. You need an eye-catching title for your ad. I always like to say Like New or Perfect condition in the title so people don't think that I am selling another beat up Craigslist item. Put the brand and Item number in the title. Don't just say, "table." People hate that crap and nobody will look at your ad. "Item Name, Item Brand, Item type, Power word, Item condition." "T.62 Stanton direct drive turntable, Perfect condition." It says everything. An expert of the product type can see the brand and model number. A novice can see the item type and brand. In the body or description of the item, you need to sound happy. "I have one perfect condition direct drive turntable for sale. The Stanton T.62 is a great turntable that will never let you down! I only used it a few times but it worked better than I could have ever imagined! You are really going to love it. It comes with the original box and all of the original accessories! If you have any questions please don't hesitate to reach out to me over phone: call, text or email." If you make products, always say brand new. Even if your product is a piece of wood cut in half to make a coaster, it is still a new coaster from the manufacturer, you.

Craigslist is best for large products and services.

Craigslist is also one of the best places to buy items for your hobby. If you like making crafts Hobby Lobby would love to sell you everything at an outrageous inflated price. Someone on Craigslist has got it for sale for much cheaper. If they don't, EBay does. Don't ever pay retail for anything. That $1000 TV you want is only $550 on Craigslist because some hillbilly can't figure out how to turn the damn thing on and wants it out of his house. Trade for it! You make dream catchers but want a new couch? Maybe someone will wheel and deal to get rid of theirs because they want their nightmares gone! This is what the Barter section is for. I highly recommend placing your product or service in the regular, for sale or service section that it aligns with and making a second listing just for the barter section. People want your stuff, show it to them in as many ways as possible.

Amazon:

Amazon is great to reach people globally. Amazon is for small products that are brand new and have a barcode. I don't sell anything on Amazon(other than books) because they have to be registered products with barcodes, product numbers etc. Unlike EBay and Craigslist you can't just sell "stuff" you made in your garage. You might be able to buy supplies for your hobby on Amazon but I think you will be better off looking at Craigslist or EBay for selling.

EBay:

EBay is awesome. EBay is so awesome that if something goes wrong while using EBay, they will pay you. More on that in a second. EBay is like Craigslist in the sense that you can make a listing for whatever it is that you are selling. EBay is the best if you are selling a small product globally. EBay has the same listing criteria as Craigslist with the security of Amazon. The downside to EBay is the shipping. When creating an EBay listing I recommend taking even more pictures than you would have if you were creating a Craigslist listing. Take 6 or more photos of the item itself, take a photo of all the accessories, the box it will come in, everything. In the description it is smart to add product specifications, on Craigslist this isn't necessary. Inflate your shipping cost, it will be higher than you think. The big thing EBay doesn't do a good job of is estimating the cost to ship your item, so don't trust what they think it will cost to ship. EBay takes a small percentage of your final selling price but in most cases doesn't charge you a listing fee. Read all of the disclaimers before listing, EBay has a lot of rules to keep both you and the buyers safe and it is important to be aware of them. Don't be afraid to reach out to EBay if you think something is wrong. I have sold hundreds of items on EBay and their staff has compensated me on multiple occasions when something didn't seem right. They will almost always do whatever it takes to keep you around buying and selling. Don't be afraid to ask them. EBay is best for small global Items.

EBay can and might be the best place to buy hobby materials. The only problem with buying items from EBay to do your hobby is that to get a great price, you might have to buy them in bulk. If you paint, buy your canvas material from EBay in rolls, it's cheap.

Etsy:

I'm not as crafty as I would like to be, but if I were, I'd be all over Etsy. Like EBay and Amazon, it is an online market place that distributes everywhere. Same listing rules apply but Etsy is great for gimmicky things. Etsy has a very low listing fee and they take a small percentage of the sale price. This is the place to sell your crafts. Jewelry, paintings, art of any kind, small crafts, you won't get a higher price for your stuff than Etsy.

Video Chat

If you sell a service that can be distributed online, like counseling services, do it! Skype it up! Good luck marketing that; I would recommend LinkedIn, Facebook, Twitter and a different book on how to do it.

When deciding on which service to use to buy and sell your products, my recommendation is all of them. Go call your friends and family, make an ad for Craigslist, EBay, and Etsy, hell even make an Amazon ad if you can. The key is to get your product in front of the most viewers as possible, so use the most markets possible to do so! Do your research, you might learn something.

Bonus tip: Go check out alibaba.com. They might

have just what you are looking for to get your projects started.

LESSON THREE: RESEARCH RESEARCH RESEARCH

The title doesn't say it enough. Research research research research. Ok that's enough to get the point across. The biggest step to turn your hobby into a money making opportunity is research! What do you need to research you ask? Everything. Who would want what you make, where do they search, how much would they pay, are there any alternatives, what is the price of the alternatives, etc.. You need to be the expert before you start.

The first thing necessary to sell your art (hobby) is how to turn your art into a product. Are you a singer? If so you need to either make a CD to sell or decide if you are going to sing live as a service. Do you make something? You need to find out how to package the items you are making for shipments or delivery. Do the research to find out what it will take to make your product purchasable. The best way to do this is to find similar products and see how other people did it. If you make furniture, go online and see what other home made furniture, that is selling online, looks like. Do they upholster it? Do they paint or stain it? Do they ship it to their customers? Do people pick it up from where it is made? You need to answer all of these questions about your product before you choose to sell it. Can your product or service even be sold? Remember if you are good at something, you can always be a guide. Do you like hiking? Give guided hiking tours at your favorite hiking location. If you want to make quilts, go to a quilt manufacturer and take a free tour. You will learn a lot about it and it may potentially teach you how to market your product, or produce it more efficiently.

You don't have anything to sell if nobody wants to buy it. Ever hear the customer is always right? I like to say the customer is always right, unless they are wrong. This is your hobby remember? Only sell it if it is still fun to make. If you are selling something you don't enjoy making, that is a job. All that being said, it is important to learn what your potential customer needs from you. This could dramatically change the outcome of your sales. If the color red is in and everyone wants a bunch of pallet furniture painted red, you better learn that so you can paint your crap red before selling it. Does your customer like Christmas songs? Make a Christmas song album. Literally ask people. You can go online and see trends and see what other sellers are doing but the best way to find what your customers might want is to ask people. Go find a blog or forum related to your hobby and ask people what they think. Go to your local markets and ask people. Get on Facebook and ask people. This is market research down to the basics, and it works. The best thing you can do is offer some sort of customization. Sell the unfinished products with options to finish them in a way that the customer wants! People love knowing that something was made just for them. The problem with customizing things is that people will start making outrageous requests so set a limit and set it very clearly. You aren't a manufacturing facility, you are a hobbyist, for now.

Where do your customers hang out? Are they hipsters that only shop on Etsy? Go sell on Etsy. Do people want you to teach their kids to bicycle? Go to biking events with fliers. Go to parks and post fliers. Give fliers to parents that you meet. Go to where your customer is. Your customer isn't sitting at home waiting for your product to show up on their Amazon wish list. You need to go out and find them. A lot of time your customer is located somewhere you have never even heard of. How do you find the then? You network. You don't know me, I don't know you, but I do know some people that might want to buy your product. Get to know me, maybe I will share these potential customers with you. The more people you know the better. It doesn't matter if the people you are meeting and networking with want to buy what you have, they have friends and family who do want to buy what you have and they will lead you straight to them. Networking is a huge part of all of my books because it is probably the most important life skill on the planet. Networking opens doors that no other skill can. Find your customer through your network. Find your customer and learn as much about them as possible. Find out where they want to shop for your product. Once you know that, that is where you sell your product.

Let's say that you've got your product on the shelves of EBay and Craigslist and you've sold a couple. That's great, but the research isn't over yet. You need feedback. You can always do something better the second, third and fourth time. Once again you need to reach out to your customers. Try and learn what they like about your service and what they don't like. Everyone likes an involved business. I've never been mad when a manager came up and asked me how my experience was at a restaurant. Do the same thing with what you are selling. How do you like the hiking tour so far? What would have made the experience even better? Would you recommend this experience to your friends? Why or why not? That's the best question: Why. Always ask why. People could say "I would prefer the quilt to be red," but why do they want it to be red? Maybe that person just likes red, or maybe they say that red is really popular right now and they think a lot of people are looking for red quilts. Boom, you just learned how to sell more quilts! Feedback is great! Be personal about it, surveys suck. Do you ever go online and take the survey on the bottom of your Walmart receipt? I haven't, but I have told a manager about my experience when they asked me face to face. Just ask, people love talking and telling their stories.

Speaking of telling stories, here's mine and how I do research. My hobby is woodworking, remember? The best way for me to package and sell my product is locally without changes or packaging. I want potential customers to be able to interact with the product when they see it, so it can't be all packaged up when they get to my woodshop. I am not creative enough to put specialty requests on the products so I don't offer any customizations. I have to sell locally because the shipping on furniture would be ridiculously expensive. Trust me I've tried to ship furniture from an EBay sale and it didn't go well. I do, however, get to learn what types of furniture people like to buy. In my case the only thing I am ok at making is desks. Believe me, if I could make chairs I would. Based on this information I sell my desks on Craigslist. Then I ask my customer what they would have liked better about the desk, after they purchase it. Using Craigslist, I can't contact my customer months later, so I try to get as much information as possible right there on the spot.

I hadn't developed my art of "hobby to money" at the time, but I did do most of these procedures when I taught swim lessons. I knew my customers were going to be parents of swimmers. I knew they would be located at pools when their kids were swimming. I presented my idea to them using fliers at the locations I knew they would be at. After I had given a lesson I would always ask if there were any other services I could be providing or anything they would like me to do differently. A lot of the time it would be easy stuff like, "she wants to work on kicking, do you think you could get your hands on some kickboards?" At the time I owned multiple kickboards so it was easy for me to start bringing things like that to the lessons and provide the exact experience that my customer wanted. Just listen to them, they know what they want. Do your research. You can never do too much research.

LESSON FOUR: BETTER THAN ENTREPRENEURSHIP

I view entrepreneurship as any practice that results in money in the bank increasing instead of decreasing. In my opinion, even couponing is a form of entrepreneurship. If you don't know what couponing is, that's ok. It is basically saving coupons from advertisements in the paper or other sources and making your buying decisions based on the coupons you collect. You don't have to make the next big tech startup company to be an entrepreneur. You just have to be conscious of what you are buying, how much you are buying, and if there is a better way to buy. I am going to call this practice of buying products the right way, front side entrepreneurship. Instead of selling products to get money, like most people view entrepreneurship, front side entrepreneurship is saving money when you purchase so that you don't have to make as much money to get what you want. Or, you can make just as much money, save on what you buy, and invest the left over money! You could also fund your hobbies with the extra money, just saying. For your reading pleasure and because entrepreneurship is long and obnoxious I will be referring to front side entrepreneurship as FSE.

FSE can be accomplished in many different ways. We can buy in bulk, buy at a discount, buy used, buy many and sell the rest, buy items in parts and assemble them, the options are endless. Do you have a Costco card? They are pretty dope, in a good way. Not only is the meal deal at the little restaurant up front an awesome deal but they have free samples of food all the time! The best part of Costco is that they have bulk items. Why buy 40 roles of toilet paper for $20 when you can buy 400 for $50 at Costco. That is assuming that you have the room for 400 roles of toilet paper. If you are willing to pay for more upfront, you pay less overall. Don't just trust that bulk is cheaper though, always confirm. Do your research.

Take advantage of coupons and discounts. "A penny saved is a penny earned," right? Who said that?

Benjamin Franklin I guess. It's true though! If you make $10 and spend $8 you have $2 left over. Well spending $7 instead is just like making that extra dollar, so take advantage of that! Don't throw that newspaper advertisement away! Read it and use those coupons to save money! Do your research! It might be fun to go buy a new item right now, but did you check if EBay has it for a quarter the price? EBay almost always has everything you are looking for at a fraction the price! I bought an IPhone charging cable from an Apple store one time and it cost me $30. Thirty freaking dollars. Do you know how much they sell for on EBay? $0.76 is the correct answer. You heard me right, $0.76 for an IPhone cable on EBay. Don't believe me? Go check it out. Type in IPhone cable, click on the buy it now tab, sort by lowest price plus shipping and there it is, $0.76. Buy 10 of them and sell 9 to people on Craigslist for $2 a pop. You've got a free cord and made some cash. Never pay full price for anything. Ever!

Speaking of buying 10 cables and buying bulk, people want the same useless junk that you want. Give it to them, with a markup. Remember how bulk is sometimes cheaper? Well if you only need one item but bulk is cheaper, buy the bulk item and sell the ones you don't need. Free items right there. FREEEEEEEE. That might be my favorite word and my favorite type of FSE. Buy low sell high. Buy lots sell what you don't need. Simple and easy to remember.

Dude, buy it used. Seriously, buy it used. Why do you need something new? What is the actual benefit of buying something new? I can't figure it out. My TV was used and it seems to have the same shows as the new TVs. It brings me the exact same amount of joy as a new TV would! The best part is that it cost me way less! I have no idea how Best Buy is still in business. If I buy a new TV, it will be from EBay. I won't ever buy a new TV, but I am just saying if I did, that is where I would buy it. I buy my TVs, and everything else for that matter, used and on Craigslist. How do I know that they work? I TEST THEM. I watch them and change channels on the remote and try all the features of the TV before I buy it. No test, no money from me. Sure you might get burned every 10,000nth time, but you saved a crap ton of money from the other 9,999 times that you came out ahead. Just buy everything used and thank me later. Don't by your toilet paper used, buy that from Costco in bulk. If you are scared of Craigslist, buy it on EBay, used, with the satisfaction of the EBay guarantee. If anything, and I mean anything, goes wrong with an EBay purchase, they will give you your money back no matter what. I once bought a receiver from EBay and they messed something up on delivery so it took a really long time to get to my house. I got to keep the receiver and they gave me all my money back. How's that for service?

Go do some research. Do enough research to build the thing you want by yourself. Maybe you're like me as a kid and really want to blow out your eardrums with a car sound system. Learn how to install it and learn about all the components that you will need. Don't know where to start? YouTube can teach you anything. Between YouTube and Wikipedia there is more knowledge than all the universities in the world combined. The best part is that they are both free to use! Take a theoretical YouTube course and learn what it takes to buy your dream items cheap. Real cheap. Hell, learn enough to start buying the parts and selling the products. That isn't FSE that's actual entrepreneurship.

To live and to practice your hobby you will need to buy things, just buy them right. None of this, "I want it now" crap, you can wait. Be patient and do research, those alone will make you wealthy with FSE. It doesn't hurt to do a little investing with that saved money, just to insure you are making extra money.

LESSON FIVE: START A BUSINESS

Ok you've done some research, you've got a hobby, you did some more research, you sold your hobby, you conducted even more research, you know how to buy the materials at the right price, now what? It pretty much sounds like you are running a small business on the side of your career. Why not make it official? You don't need a lawyer, you don't need an HR department, you don't even need employees. You just need a name, a website, some business cards, and the government's approval. It's pretty easy and has a bunch of benefits.

So you're trying to come up with a name? Tough right? I started a home remodeling business and it took me forever to come up with the name. I asked everyone I knew if they had any ideas, I even dreamed about names at night, I eventually settled on Home Again Renovations LLC. The name is way too long, but you deal with the options you have. Try telling people your email address that ends with @homeagainrenovations.com. Takes a whole business card just to write the freaking name on it. Don't make my mistake, make it short. There are two very important factors you need to consider when picking a name. The first is if the name is available according to the government. Most states have a website that you can type in the desired name and it will tell you if the name is available or not. Pretty simple, don't pick one that is taken, it won't get approved. The second thing to consider is the domain name. You should pick a name that has an available domain that matches, or is at least close to, the business name. It is also ok an abbreviation of the name is available to use that. Just pick something that isn't too far from the available domain name.

You need a website; it is crucial to your success. I don't think I need to explain to you why a website is extremely important to a business. Just in case you live under a rock and that rock blocks Wi-Fi and phone signals I'll tell you anyway. A website establishes credibility for potential customers. A website markets your product. A website puts you in contact with customers. A website gives you an email with your domain name. A website gives you a tool to teach people more about your business. A website is vital and there is no reason to go without one. A domain name generally costs $15 or so. There are many companies on the web that offer free templates that you simply apply to your domain and then drag and drop your pictures and themes to get the general layout of your website. There are no excuses for not having a website. Everything is user friendly and cheap.

You will use your website later on to do more research on your customers. You can even use your website to host or sell your products and services. For now, make sure that you have an about us page, a landing page, a contact us page, a testimonials or past projects page, and maybe even a blog page. Do not make your website complicated and in depth. Everything should be easy to read and easy to access. The main goal of the website, like all tools you add to your business, is to sell more products. Make that easier for your customers by giving them a clear and easy path to buy. Simple is better.

Go get business cards. Vistaprint.com is cheap, user-friendly, and gets the job done. I don't care who you use but for less than $10 you can have a thousand cards ready to hand to your potential customers. Once again the goal is to generate more sales so skip the colorful BS and give them the information they need to know: your name, contact information, and ohhh ya that awesome website you have. Make the path to buying very clear on your business card. I like to leave the back of my business cards blank so that I can write additional or specific information on the back. This is a great networking tool. If you can write something specific about the conversation you are having with someone on the back of the card, they are more likely to remember you when they look at the card. Network network network.

Ready for some boring details?

The same website that you discovered your business name availability from the government will most likely be the place to register your business. It is as simple as picking out a name that is available, paying $100, and picking the business type. The business types available at this stage of your business are sole proprietorship, corporation, and LLC. There are other types, many other types, but most of them don't apply to this type of business. If you want a partner, there are also partner versions of the government legal structures I just mentioned. A sole proprietorship is the most basic of the three. It basically means that you, as an individual, are selling products or services on your own. You will use your own bank accounts, your own taxes, and you will take on the liability on your own. This is no different than just being a person and selling a product without a business. The benefit of a sole proprietorship is the simplicity of the structure. You and the business are one entity. You can still write business expenses off on your taxes but you are responsible for any and all costs that the company might take on. If the company goes into bankruptcy, you are in bankruptcy. The partnership version of a sole proprietorship is called just that, a partnership.

The second type is a corporation. A corporation is like a person of its own. A corporation can have its own bank accounts, it can own its own property, and it takes on the liability. Multiple people can own portions of the corporation. This is the most complex structure of the three because it is basically another human being in the eyes of the government. They are taxed on their own, they have rights of their own, and owners of the business can change all the time. I do not recommend this type of company structure because of the complicated maintenance it requires to operate. I would highly suggest meeting with a lawyer and a CPA before forming a corporation.

The third type, and my favorite type, is a limited liability company. AN LLC is like a hybrid of the other two types. It is simple and can be managed as easily as a sole proprietorship, but also provides some of the great amenities that a corporation brings to the table. AN LLC separates the owner or owners from the company just enough to allow the business to have its own bank accounts and take on its own liability. If an individual wanted to sue your company, they can only take what the company owns, not the owners personal net worth, in most cases. A sole proprietorship however can be sued for the full value of the owner's net worth because the company and the individual are one and the same. Go for the LLC; it isn't complicated and it protects you from most threats that would take down your business.

Generally, a CPA or certified public accountant will be willing to explain all of these in more detail for free if you use them when it comes to tax season. Use this to make your choice.

Ok we made it through the dense stuff, let's lighten it up a bit. What are the benefits to owning a business anyway? On top of separating yourself from the business for security reasons that I just explained, it also opens up a lot of money saving doors. If you own a business, all of your expenses that you incur to create your product or service are tax deductible. That is, if you spend $20 to make a product that sells for $30, you are only taxed for the $10 difference. The best part of this is that your car, your office, your pens and paper, they are all considered expenses. You need your car to go to the supply store to buy supplies, your car is part of the business. You need stamps to ship things to clients. A lot of things in your life can be dual purposed for your personal life and for the business, but they are still business expenses. You aren't getting these items for free, but you do get to claim that you are making less profit, therefore you pay less in taxes. This can be a little confusing so let's use some fake numbers to create an example.

Before you were a business owner you spent $10,000 a year owning and operating a car, $500 on shipping supplies, and $5,000 to keep a storage unit for your hobbies. You then create An LLC for the multiple awesome reasons listed above. That year you get to claim that on top of the individual cost of your products, you also incurred $15,500 in fixed business expenses. If you made $14,000 that year from your hobby, you have a net difference of negative $1,500. You don't have to pay any taxes for your business that year because you "lost money." In reality, you would have had to have a car and you would have kept that storage unit even if you didn't run the business. In that case you would have made a profit of $14,000 and you would have to pay taxes on all $14,000 of profit you made. See the benefit? If you are in the 30% tax bracket that comes out to a $4,200 savings just by starting an LLC.

That is, if you would have paid taxes on your hobby in the first place. If you are just a small time hobbyist selling a few items a year, I wouldn't bother setting up a business because the government isn't going to bother you for making $300 a year on craft sales. It all depends on if you want to grow your hobby into a business or not.

LESSON SIX: COMPETITION

If you are growing your hobby into a business you will eventually run into competition. A joke to keep it light: What is big and strong and always innovating? Your competition. That wasn't funny at all was it? Maybe my comedian career hasn't taken off yet. Do you know what has taken off? The knock off of your product. That was a little better right? If you start doing something right other people will want to do what you are doing, and they will be successful at it. Chances are that your business is just a knock off of someone else's. Unless you are providing a new drug or an extremely innovative technology company, you are probably providing a product that someone else is already selling. When I taught swim lessons I knew there were other instructors out there, better instructors out there. This didn't stop me because I knew then and I know now; there is room for all of us. It is still fun to win right? So, what can you do to beat the market? This is where your marketing team comes into play. You're a hobbyist running a business, you are the marketing team.

Everyone looks to price first. When I was developing my swim lesson business I didn't know any better and went straight for the lowest price. Did this strategy get me clients? Yes, it did but it was all short term and in the end the business failed. Because I had a low price many people saw this as an opportunity to get lessons for their kid for a cheap price and jumped on board. In the end however, the top swimmers still went to the more expensive teachers. Because I wasn't teaching any of the top swimmers I was viewed as a discount service, not a premium service. Parents especially want to give their kids the best opportunities as possible and in the end everyone wanted the better instructor. Even if I was the better coach, my price made me look like a cheap alternative. Price will get you some customers up front, it will not buy a long term relationship, it will not give you a good reputation.

Service service service! I spent a couple of years as a salesman for a large lumber distributor. Sales is hard. A lot of people think that salesman just play golf and eat food with their customers all day. There is a little bit of truth to this but I would say maybe 1% truth. Those luxuries are just a little bribe to open a potential client's ears. The true task and the other 99% of the job is convincing a customer that you are better than the competition. This is the language of service. Do you think I would have such high praise for EBay if they hadn't refunded my money so many times when things went south? No way. It is their security, a service they provide, that keeps me coming back. EBay could have the lowest price in town every time but if you got burnt on every other order you would never use them.

You need to have better service than your competition. Every single time, pick up the phone as quickly as possible. If you miss a call, call them back as quickly as possible. The biggest thing is to keep your promises. If you create an expected deadline, make it happen. "I can get that dream catcher to you by Wednesday." You better freaking have that dream catcher in the hands of that customer by Wednesday. If you don't, do you know the first thing they will say to their friends about your businesses? "So and so took a million years to get this POS delivered to me." Even if you have the best product in the world, it doesn't matter if your service sucks.

The only companies that you keep going back to with bad service are the ones you have to. Think about it, your internet provider is a jerk and you know it. You can't go anywhere else though. That is the only reason they can get away with that. Companies that are dependent on their customers all have to provide amazing service. Even the retail god Walmart will take back any product you want to return. They don't do it out of the good graces of their heart, they do it because they have to, to keep you as a customer. Set service goals that will blow your competition out of the water and meet every single one of them. It is better to set a lower goal and make it, when it comes to service, than to give the customer a wrong expectation. Customers expectations are set by what you tell them to be. If you say that it takes 3 weeks to make a dream catcher, they think it takes three weeks. If your competition can do it in 1 week, you better do some more research.

There's that word again, research. Who knows your competition? Their customers. People are willing to tell you what they don't like. People also love to bitch and moan about all the awful things going on in their lives and your competition is one of them. Ask those people what they like and don't like about your competition, I bet they would love to tell you. Not only is this a great way to learn how to grow and improve your business, it is also a great way to let a potential customer open up. When a prospect opens up, they are giving some of their trust to you. The more a customer trusts you, the more likely they are to buy from you. Selling is like dating. You don't just go all the way on the first date, you open up to each other and eventually build a partnership that benefits both you and your customers. They are loyal to you, you are loyal to them, it's a great relationship.

You can also read about your competition on their WEBSITE. If they don't have a website, check out their product listing on EBay or Amazon. The web is a public display of information and they are giving out huge amounts of information in hopes to snag a customer. This information is also a great way to understand their approach to finding customers and how they operate as a business. Use this information to shape your business.

Innovating and pivoting might be the most important way to stay ahead of competition, but they are so important let's give them their own chapters.

Not all competition is bad. In fact, competition

promotes growth and innovation. There are plenty of fish in the sea, don't let the fact that anther business is doing what you want to do stop you from accomplishing your goals. Go out there and get what you deserve!

LESSON SEVEN: PIVOT AND INNOVATE

Pivoting is a very common term in the business world. Just like in basketball pivoting is keeping one foot planted, while simultaneously moving in another direction. I think you know what innovating means right? If not, I'll let you look that one up on your own. Before we dive too deep into these two terms I want to tell you about another famous business theory.

The theory is called the ugly baby syndrome. All parents love their children right? I hope you answered yes to that, if not, got read my other book *How To Get A job and Move Out of Your Parent's Basement.* Use the tips on how to separate yourself from needy family members. Anyway, parents love their children. Parents love their child even if the kid is an extremely ugly baby. A business is like a child to a business owner. You create it from nothing, nurture it to life, and help it grow, until eventually you die and your business becomes wildly successful after you are gone. Maybe not exactly like that but you get the point. People have a really hard time differentiating a good idea from a bad one when they have spent an enormous amount of time developing it. AKA the ugly baby syndrome. You may think you have created the best business idea ever, your baby, but everyone else just sees a really ugly baby, or a bad idea. Luckily, if you can get passed the fact that your idea sucks, you can pivot and innovate.

In the business world, if you aren't growing, you are dying. Time to get out there and grow! How do you grow? You come up with new wonderful advancements in your product lines and services. You aren't just a piano teacher, you are a piano teacher that turns the student's performances into fancy light shows and something else cool. Let's try again, you aren't just a painter, your paintings also come with a 30-page written story that deeply moves the reader and brings more meaning to the piece of art. Both of those examples suck but I think you get the point. Create the IPod, then create the IPhone, then create the IPad. Do not stop innovating or you will fall over and lose to the competition who is innovating.

You own a HD flat screen TV right? Why did you buy this TV? Because it had better features than your previous TV? These are innovations. Chances are that your previous TV was even the same brand as your new TV. You need to continuously adapt your product or service to better fit the needs of your customers. Sometimes the needs of your customer's changes drastically. Or even better yet sometimes your ideas are dumb and you need a better product all together. This is where pivoting comes in.

Sony didn't get up and stop making TV's when the needs of their customers changed to tablets, the pivoted to make tablets as well. They kept one foot firmly planted in the TV market, making innovations to that product line but still planted in TVs. They then moved their other foot into a completely different market, tablets. By keeping one foot in TVs they get to keep all of their current and repeat customers. They aren't risking their entire business on a new idea. Who knows, the new idea could be an ugly baby. They have their established working business in TVs, still running smoothly, and they are taking a small risk in the tablet market. Now that the tablet market is extremely successful they can add that to their existing business model and try and pivot their risk foot to another idea. A company like Sony might have 50 legs, so pivoting is much easier for them. If you only have one product, pivoting is difficult because a table with one leg doesn't stand for very long. Diversify your company's product lines and services to reduce risk.

Sometimes a company also needs to pivot away from a product, service, or product line. Remember pagers? If you are producing pagers, it might be time to pivot away from that product line. In this instance you would be picking up your back foot and either moving and focusing on what you are successful at or trying a new product or service line. The important thing is that you do not stick to a failing business just because it made you money in the past. Everything is moving and changing and your business needs to move and change to keep up. Actually, don't keep up, stay ahead of the curve. Beat your competition to the punch. Early adopters of new products spend way more per product than regular consumers. Create the new product or service before it exists and you make boatloads of money.

So, who decides when it is time to pivot? Well ya, technically you make the choice in the end but really it is your customers. This is where, once again, all that research and learning from your customers comes in. Your customers will express their wants and needs and you need to pivot and innovate to fulfill those needs. "But Spencer, nobody was going around asking Apple to come up with the IPad." This is true, but customers were loving the new IPhone innovation and people were trying to get away from their computers and smart phones just weren't cutting it. Apple listened to the customers needs and developed a product to fit those needs. Customers wanted the power of laptops with the convenience of smart phones. Back to TVs. Customers are always demanding higher and higher resolution. TV companies just keep making higher and higher resolution TVs. When Sony thought they could take the market with 3D TVs, even though the customers didn't care about 3D, they failed. Do you know what did take off that Sony instigated? The 4K TV. AKA just another jump in resolution like the customers were asking for. Listen to your customers needs, that will lead you in the right direction.

LESSON EIGHT: DIVERSIFY

Diversify your life! Make friends with different cultures! Try things you've never done before. See and experience whole new worlds. Get new hobbies, quit jobs, start businesses, do literally everything! Except meth, remember, don't do meth. Anyway... Diversify everything, including your hobbies. Why have one hobby when you can have four? Why have a small network when you can have a large network? Go do something that makes you uncomfortable. Why should you diversify? Two reasons: experience and safety.

Have you heard the phrase diversifying your portfolio reduces risk? Do you know why it reduces risk? Not to go into too much detail or repeat myself too much, but basically the more you are involved in, the less likely one failure will affect you. If you own ten businesses and one fails, you still own nine businesses. If you own one business and that one business fails, you have zero businesses. Simple right? Did you ever wonder why CEO's are on the boards of many different companies? Well, on top of being involved in many different things and all the fun and experience that comes along with that, they are diversifying their portfolios.

So how do you successfully diversify? You really need to branch out. I mean really far out. If you own ten companies and all ten of them are oil companies, that isn't diversifying. What happens if the oil industry falls off the face of the Earth? You don't own any companies. One oil company, two tech companies, a couple banks, a food distributor, some insurance companies and fill the rest with retail stores. That is a much better example of diversifying.

How does this apply to us? We can diversify in a couple different ways. The first is by offering multiple products or services. The second is by turning multiple hobbies into successful money making opportunities. The third is by going out and experiencing new things in our personal lives.

We talked about pivoting before and this is the most effective way to diversify within your business. It allows you to pick up new products or services while still relying on what you do best. If your industry allows, pick up as many products and services as possible to add to your businesses portfolio. If you sell hammocks it probably doesn't make much sense to also sell TV's through the same business. Don't get me wrong, if the two are related and it is easy to do, more power to you! But, it might be easier to sell hammocks and t-shirts because they use similar materials and processes. This is why shoe companies make shirts and socks. This is why car companies make many different models. They are all diversifying as much as they can with similar processed goods and resources.

Let's say that you want to sell hammocks and TV's are you just out of luck? No way! You need two ventures! Why not have a business/hobby for making hammocks and a business for selling TV's? maybe you'll grow enough to get an employee, wouldn't that be cool! But seriously, what if all the hippies fall off the face of the Earth and the hammock market crashes? You've still got your TV market to rely on. Go start a bunch of businesses! What's the worst that can happen? Well, do

"Luck is what happens when preparation meets opportunity." –Seneca the Younger. All you have to do is put yourself out there and people will present you with opportunities. If you do your research, research, research you will be more than prepared to take advantage of all of them. Network because people provide opportunities, and people create the future.

LESSON NINE: MANAGE YOUR PORTFOLIO

You've learned the skills necessary to lead and innovate by growing your hobbies into successful money making businesses. Now it is time to sit back and relax while you watch your bank account overflow. Wait, you need to manage your businesses? Well that's a bummer. Ohhh wait, it's actually a lot of fun? Ok I'm in. If you don't manage your businesses continuously, they will fall apart like my swim lesson business and car audio businesses did. I was young and "dumb" and I have no regret letting those fall apart, but I want my current ventures and future ventures to succeed forever. As I mentioned earlier, I run a small remodeling and investment property business and it needs constant watch. I am the only full time employee of the business so I don't need to keep an eye out for anyone else at this point, but if I do not monitor the website and emails I will miss all the opportunities to grow. Once again, if a business isn't growing, it is dying. I make it a priority to do what I call system checks every day. There are a few things I do every morning when I first wake up and right before I go to bed each day to make sure I am not missing any opportunities.

System check one: I check my 4 different emails, EBay, LinkedIn and Facebook in that order, the moment I wake up in the morning. If there is a potential client or request, I will hear about it through email or text. If any of them need further action, I mark them. Only once I have solved the problem or helped the customer do I remove the mark. I never delete emails because you never know when you might need that little piece of communication for liability reasons. Mark them as unread, flagged, whatever you have to do to tell yourself action is still needed, but never delete them. Learning everything I need to do to make my customers happy first thing in the morning helps me plan my day. If I can respond or help a customer right then and there, I do it. The faster I respond, the better service I am providing.

Next is EBay. I check if anything has sold because I

might need to fit a post office run into my schedule. This time also allows me to do a little market research on how my products are doing and if there are any changes I need to make to help them sell faster.

Social media is next. Like I said, people create opportunities, I do not want to be delayed when responding to a potential opportunity. Go add me on LinkedIn, I'd love to network with you. Tell me how fast my response time is! I love feedback.

System check two: After getting ready and planning my day it is time to start solving problems. I schedule my day around completing the most projects as possible. I keep my phone on me during the day to make sure I still get email and EBay notifications. I leave enough open room in my day to solve emergency problems if they come up throughout the day. I check on all of my projects during this time. If it is a house for sale or something that doesn't change as often, I wont check on it every day but I definitely check on it once a week.

System check three: During lunch I do a second scan over the emails I have received throughout the day to make sure I have solved or plan to solve everything that needs further action. I should mention, I write everything down that I need to get done on a piece of paper. It may be old school but I love the feeling of crossing items off the list once I have completed them. The other benefit to writing everything I need to get done on a piece of paper is that I can clearly see everything I have finished and everything I still need to get done.

System check four: Similar to system check two, I use this portion to run the operations and logistics of my different ventures but I still keep my notifications on so I can hear if an emergency comes up.

System check Five: I do an end of the day check. I go back to all of my emails and confirm that everything made it to the paper list and everything on the list was marked off. I check my listings and see if there are any last minute actions I need to take or if anything will need to be done the next day. Finally, I check social media, specifically LinkedIn, so that I can stay in touch with my network.

System check six: I continue to keep my phone on me throughout the night so that I can respond to anyone with concerns and so that I can keep an eye out for potential emergencies.

Because I do multiple scans over the different sources that I use to reach out to my customers, I have a low likelihood of missing something important. Once again the whole point of checking multiple times is to make sure I do not miss a single opportunity. I do not want any of my businesses to fall through the cracks, so I monitor them constantly. Watch trends in sales and make sure to listen to feedback. These will help you decide which direction your different businesses need to head in. Don't let anything fall between the cracks, writing things down always helps me make sure I don't miss a single thing. I call my paper the goal sheet. I love crushing goals and this makes me feel like I knock goals out of the park every day. You don't have to be as structured about it as I am but I do highly recommend a regular organizations system. Go have fun!

LESSON TEN: THE STEPS

Need a recap? Ya me too. Here we go, everything needed to turn your hobby into a money making machine.

Step one: Get a hobby.

I hope you already have a hobby, but if you don't I think it is about time to go out and get one. They are fun and as you learned they can make you some side cash or even turn into a successful business. Almost anything can fit into this category, fishing, running, cutting trees, building desks, whatever you are into, so is someone else.

Step two: Learn your market.

It is simple and easy to learn where your product or service can be sold. Is it a large product? Don't go somewhere that needs shipping. Is your service face to face? Don't offer it on EBay, this step is pretty much common sense. Learn as much as you can about each market and you will make the right choice.

Step three: Learn your product/service.

You can't learn too much. Do more research than anyone, be the expert. Listen and learn from potential customers. They know what they want and how they want it. Give them what they want. Your customers are more than willing to tell you what they want, you really need to listen to them. Plus, take advantage of that awesome resource, the internet!

Step four: Make the right buying choices.

It doesn't matter if you have the coolest product on the market if you can't afford to make it. Learn the art of buying what you need for the right price. Large companies have whole departments dedicated to buying. It is clearly important! Make it a priority. And remember FSE is key.

Step five: Why not grow?

If things seem to be taking off and you are enjoying what you do, it might be time to make a business out of your hobby. Being your own boss is fun, even if it is just for your side job. You get to watch your business grow and evolve into bigger and better things. It truly is a great experience and I hope you get to try it sometime. Go take some risks!

Step six: Competition sucks.

You will run into competition but do not fret. This is your time to shine! Price wars don't get you anywhere, beat them with service and innovation. There is nothing like the smell of victory in the morning. Go win!

Step seven: Keep it fresh.

The typewriter was one of the most innovative products of all time but is practically useless today. Don't forget to stay fresh with your business, products, and services. Don't be afraid to make moves and adapt according to your customers needs.

Step eight: Split it up.

Part of staying fresh is trying new things. I bet you haven't even found your true passion yet. You may think it's reading "how to" books by a millennial, but really it's swimming with dolphins! Who knows what it is. Only you can discover your passion by trying everything!

Step nine: Don't fall behind.

What's the point of creating something great if you are just going to sit back and watch it fail? Make sure to stay on top of your business. You love your hobby; you will love managing your hobby as a business. You have what it takes, I know it!

Step ten: Have fun.

Go enjoy what the world has to offer. Buy products from other people's hobby based businesses. Climb a mountain, go to a stand up comedian's show, start a bunch of weird businesses. Go do it all and have fun doing it.

Thank you for the read. If you enjoyed this, please go read my other books! I leave you with one last piece of advice: Appreciate Art

BONUS LESSON: APPRECIATE ART

I mean this both figuratively and literally. Art is pretty awesome. What you and I view as art might be totally different, but I want to experience your art. I enjoy painting, building and writing, all of which I consider art. I appreciate you for participating in my writing and I want to experience whatever it is that you call art. So for both of our sakes, I hope you start selling your art. If you practice something as a hobby, you are making art. Make beautiful music and share it with us! Build toys and show them to us! Hike mountains and guide us along! I want to see and hear everything that you have to offer and so does everyone else. We can make this world a healthy and beautiful one by sharing what we are truly passionate about. Help make the world a wonderful place by filling it with your creativity and individuality. As always, fund the sciences, fund the arts, and fund our futures. I'll see you in the creative paradise we build together on Earth.

Made in the USA
San Bernardino, CA
10 March 2017